TWO

TWO

The Diseased Tree

Book of Obituaries

SHAUN DeNOOYER

RESOURCE *Publications* • Eugene, Oregon

TWO
The Diseased Tree, Book of Obituaries

Copyright © 2024 Shaun DeNooyer. All rights reserved. Except for brief quotations in critical publications or reviews, no part of this book may be reproduced in any manner without prior written permission from the publisher. Write: Permissions, Wipf and Stock Publishers, 199 W. 8th Ave., Suite 3, Eugene, OR 97401.

Resource Publications
An Imprint of Wipf and Stock Publishers
199 W. 8th Ave., Suite 3
Eugene, OR 97401

www.wipfandstock.com

PAPERBACK ISBN: 979-8-3852-0452-6
HARDCOVER ISBN: 979-8-3852-0453-3
EBOOK ISBN: 979-8-3852-0454-0

02/06/24

CONTENTS

List of Abbreviations | vii

THE DISEASED TREE

BOOK OF OBITUARIES
Lucy Riser | 15
Joseph Hayfire | 16
Joshua Wanton | 18
Teddy Browning | 19
Lee Field | 21
Henry Olden | 22
Art Fieldrunner | 23
Tom Hedger | 24
John Radder | 25
Guy Tidewell | 27
Billy Wellsound | 28
Olivia Bracer | 29
Reddy Friend | 30
August Red | 32
Dillon Pool | 33
Evan Mint | 35
Eden Brush | 36

Parker Upfell | 37

Fenton Jackson | 38

Jamie Saxon | 39

Guy Peakmire | 40

Perry Overman | 41

Tarwell Hopefor | 42

Dane Ward | 43

Slade Welte | 44

Coaxer Seedtree | 45

Isabel Weatherway | 46

Alice Went | 47

Troy Idle | 48

Hugo Betty | 49

Midnight Genesis | 50

LIST OF ABBREVIATIONS

R & R   rest and relaxation

THE DISEASED TREE

God never looks up

The Nachash in the garden
Tempted our first parents, who
Chose to disobey God and
Thereby brought death to us all.

We are a people crying from the
Borderlands of hell, seething writhing
Monsters fearing for survival in the
Jungles of our minds, our hearts
Pumping the sludge of wickedness
Like venom in the blood
Of frightened predators.

We are a depraved people, bathing
In the fountain of evil, scrubbing
With lust, and trudging through
The deserts of the Africa of our
Souls, ever bellowing the song of
Spiritual disharmony.

The blood is not only a body-river
Transporting breath-cargo through
Essential vessels for earthly life,
But 'tis that which connects us all
To our progenitor.
Whether or not you think the
Tarnishes are obvious, sin has
Enslaved me, and it enslaves you.
No self-inspection may come to
Know what is housed
In thine own heart.

Regarding the terminal permanence
Of the disobedience of man, and the
Climate therein: fact: man sinned.
And because of this transgression,
Every man from Adam will sin.
And as natural man is self-guided
By the compass of pride, were it not
For common grace, every encounter
Would be an encounter with
Unrestrained evil.

There are no spiritually maimed.
All are bulging-eye dead, spiritually:
Vainglorious conquistadors with
Pride-cooked hearts and
Dagger-pointing wills.

Sin was the scream that awakened
The beast of death.
Physical death, yes.
But also, spiritual death—life
Without life.

All have sinned and fall short of the glory of God.

Rom 3:23

Therefore, there's no
Such thing as a good person.
All are evil.
And most will perish.

For the gate is narrow and the way
is hard that leads to life, and those
who find it are few.

Matt 7:14

Justice is a hard and final answer to
Idolatry, murder, rape, thieving,
Lying, adultery, gossiping, etc.

The wrath of God must be satisfied.
Alas, hell is the rightful answer to
Such rebellion to our creator.

Every human life is either a fast
Or slow destruction.
And destruction is not always
Outwardly chaotic, but is
Sometimes quietly vampiric, as the
Unregenerate man is drained by the
Offerings of the world until all that
Remains is the irremovable mark.

Worldly distractions distract you
Daily until you die.
And the distractions of the world
Bring only a slight reprieve to loss
And despair.
And the world distracts you with
Self-improvement, traveling,
Careers, money, sex, stardom,
Media, art, social justice,
And humanitarianism.

Anything to keep you from
Thinking about truth.
Nothing the unregenerate man
Achieves, will ever quell
Even a jot of his despair.

The Devil stokes the fire of your
Heart with the lie that what you
Think will help you, grow you,
Advance you, enlighten you,
Save you, will.

The most dangerous thing a man
Can do is follow his heart, for the
Heart is a violet flame of perverse
Desire, a wholly ravenous thing.

The heart is deceitful above all things, and desperately sick; who can understand it?

Jer 17:9

The unregenerate man believes his
Hopes and dreams are noble endeavors,
But they are, in truth,
Nothing more than self-advocated
Surrender to the world.
And the world has no answers.
And there are no answers within.
And escaping yourself is
An impossibility.

In a world full of wickedness and
Rebellion, the stronger man's will
Becomes, the more lost he becomes.
For the will of man is the
Death of hope.

Do you think that each one of us
Holds one of the many answers to
One of the many questions on how
To progress civilization? Nay:

Claiming to be wise, they became fools, and exchanged the glory
of the immortal God for images resembling mortal man and
birds and animals and creeping things. Therefore God gave them
up in the lusts of their hearts to impurity, to the dishonoring of
their bodies among themselves, because they exchanged the truth
about God for a lie and worshiped and served the creature rather
than the Creator, who is blessed forever! Amen.

Rom 1:22–25

There are those who have actual wisdom:
Something so bright as to create a
Thousand shadows around them.
And then there are others, whose
Proclaimed wisdoms run like the romp
And roar of a wild cub until foolishly
Staggering into the mouth
Of a mightier animal.

Until one undergoes the transformation
Of the remission of sins, what we think
We know shall remain hidden like

Hieroglyphics plastered throughout the
Deepest sub-regions of the world.

The unregenerate man knows nothing of
The war that is raging, and being
Fought in the name and authority of
The Lord Jesus Christ by plainclothes
Warriors against the evil
In the spiritual realm.

For we wrestle not against flesh and blood, but against principalities, against powers, against the rulers of the darkness of this world, against spiritual wickedness in high places.

Eph 6:12

A great man, in the eyes of the world,
Is the captain of his soul, capable of
Spectacular feats and reaching new
Regions of reality.
In truth, the mast of his pride has
Caused irreparable damage to the hull
Of his being, routing his vessel
Towards eternal, outer darkness.
The gravity of life is stronger than
The gravity of death, for death has
Been conquered by
The cross-work of Christ.
But the unregenerate man, in his
Rebellion against God, seeks to, and
Will continue to seek, to eradicate
Death as a substitute for salvation.

But God will not be mocked.
For God is a consuming fire, and, as
Everything but Christ is a heap of
Falsity, the flame of truth shall
Leave but ashes of lies.

One sin against a holy God
Condemns the sinner to the lake
Of fire, separating him from his
Maker for all eternity.

We are enslaved to sin: deceitful,
Haughty, boastful, malicious, etc.

Therefore, what can man offer
A holy God?

Nothing.

What do we deserve?

Hell.

The glorious Good News:
Jesus Christ came to earth on a rescue mission to save sinners. The holy Son of God (God incarnate born of a virgin) lived a sinless life that we could never live, and willingly sacrificed himself as the unblemished lamb to appease his Father's righteous and terrible wrath.

Why?

Love.

Unfathomable love.

But he was pierced for our transgressions; he was crushed for our iniquities; upon him was the chastisement that brought us peace, and with his wounds we are healed. All we like sheep have gone astray; we have turned—every one—to his own way; and the Lord has laid on him the iniquity of us all.

Isa 53:5–6

For our sake he made him to be sin who knew no sin, so that in him we might become the righteousness of God.

2 Cor 5:21

BOOK OF OBITUARIES

LUCY RISER

Lucy was born in 1909 in Boston, Massachusetts. Died in 1952 in New York City. Stern parents. Strife at school. Ridicule. The bobbed haircut came in her twenties. So did the theatrical hatred and the dramatic violence. She was a flapper-wife. Dance halls and alcohol. Did the deed more than him. She was a stardom seeker. Auditions and abortions. Relished in praise. Torn lingerie. Her beauty was the type that would linger for a good long time in the mind, but only to those who remained no more than a peripheral thing in her life. Lucy's life, in her mind, was the very life of life. Everything else: a husband, a lover, a friend, a tree, a soda pop: a prop.

JOSEPH HAYFIRE

Joseph was born in 1944 in New Orleans, Louisiana. Died in 1993 in New Orleans, Louisiana. His parents were harsh disciplinarians. Iron father. Bladed mother. Joseph's father was the kind of person closest to being right if you were always wrong. Joseph's mother masked her misery with many masks, but masks are masks, and thus were these masks just other kinds of ugly. Joseph thought a lot about things. And Joseph thought what was kept in his mind was kept there for the same reason things are packed before trips are taken. When Joseph had come of age, he began to have issues relating to his friends. Most things did not affect him like others, nor were they the crucial what that he thought of when thinking of what he should be doing. Discomfort was strong. It was about at this time in his life when a friend from school invited him to go to church. He went. Was given a Bible. Would frequently read it. He would hide it at first. From his parents. And from kids at school. But eventually he read it openly. At home. And other places too. He didn't feel ashamed when his friends ridiculed him. Or when his dad laughed about him becoming a preacher. And on the day that school let out, summer 1960, Joseph prayed a cavalier prayer: Lord, if you hear me, please give me lightning passion and thunderous vigor. Let me draw devastating interest to myself so that I may be of good use to you. The years past, darkly. And his days were dim. And the stars were sores upon his psyche. The mightiness of God worked upon his lofty, desire-laden heart until that high-rise pride fell to a glorious destruction. And when Joseph finally repented, repent he did like a well without an ounce of moisture. It was as if a great veering had happened. For the drought of his being had been, and would continue to be, quenched by the eternal wellspring of the love of Christ. His way was different. He Believed. And he was cross at things he wasn't before. And he was loving towards those he couldn't never been. And one day, in his roadside apartment, he ran to his kitchen, and on a paper plate wrote thus: *is it that when a man suffers but for the sake of Christ he may come to focus his strengths on that which may lead him to introduce one to the only one who can make whole even those whose despair seems like an indecipherable hurt of the heart?*

The rest of Joseph's life was spent with men dying in the street, telling stories with twisty turns of righteousness and mercy. Henceforth did he praise God for "Road to Damascus" experiences in a Raymond Chandler setting.

JOSHUA WANTON

Joshua was born in 1926 in Detroit, Michigan. Died in 1926 in Detroit, Michigan. Delicate gestures comforted him. Fever reduced him. Joshua died in the scant arms of a caring whore in a musty brothel of the slums.

TEDDY BROWNING

Teddy was born in 1923 in Burlington, Vermont. Died in 1974 in New York City. Teddy grew up amidst the terrible mutterings of stillborn personalities. His father, a soul consumed, would sit for hours in the yard wholly entranced with dead grass. Would seek solace in the emptiness of the sky. Teddy felt his father's frustration like a piece of steel put to a bird. Storms always brought him happiness, for he would imagine that he was adventuring under the foreboding sky, ever in search of a place of his own making. Teddy was obsessed with the idea that his birth was the reason he became unknown. He wanted to be "washed" of his physical makeup into a figure bursting with light like a luminescent peacock. He wanted to witness the spits of breath of the phantoms of a new sea licking the shore of a most majestic world. Teddy was bloated with longing. With unexecuted purpose. Feeling more and more like his surroundings were but a place blown over by time, abandoned to the past, sometimes he would sit still and put his thoughts together and try to evoke a most remarkable otherworld. When he was thirteen, he went to a church alone. Church became the bedrock of his life. An after-school-before-home home. A mythology of heroes and foes. But his religiosity kept him hanging in the balance. When Teddy was fifteen, he ran away. He lived in the tunnel outside town. Teddy's idea of himself grew aggressively. The myth was launched. Teddy thought that God had surely made him with special thought. Had whispered to his soul the secrets of His cause and had thereby given him the amplest grace. Teddy's mission was to penetrate the learned and lifeless worldly people. Teddy's motto that he had written in his threadbare notebook that he read every morning was: *I bear the soul of heaven's woe for humanity. Thy soul is the bullseye for the firearm of my mind.* One night when night had fallen and there was no more light by which to see, when one no longer knows the way from which he came or the way to go, in such darkness, and in the throes of the bat-skied torment of self-discernment, unable to confront the incoherent properties of his dreams, Teddy began to truly seek the truth. And 'twas on that night when he first heard evil whisper. And this above the rest he sought to flee. In Teddy there was now an urge to follow what was intended by God to be the most pivotal reason for his existence. The realization of his disobedience to God was more clarification than the evils he saw on the news. A Godfearing man and disciple he was to be. For not a day later did he find a bible in a dumpster. And it wasn't long until the shield of self was shattered by the sword of truth. His last years were spent on a street corner preaching the baptism of fire. For such was the power of his conviction that the Good News was brought to many.

LEE FIELD

Lee was born in 1941 in Chattanooga, Tennessee. Died in 1967 in Memphis, Tennessee. Lee grew up in the seediest section of the wrong side of the tracks. Lee's father took care of lawns. Lee's mother sold casseroles and handed out tracts. Both of Lee's parents loved Jesus strongly. Spoke much of atonement and destiny. Growing up, Lee's mother had taught him that the soul is the carrier of spiritual cargo, and the contents, if not proclaimed by Christ, were far beyond a threat to the state of the soul. She would say things like, "Man is dissociated from any sense of identity, for he is hypnotized in a sinful slumber." But Lee never took his mother seriously. And he wasn't impressed with most people. He was as indifferent to the words of his mother as a moody babysitter. But when the cost of manhood came to cost him nearly all was when he sought for the absolute. And with more and more of scripture, more testimonies, and the more lighted he was with true light, Lee began to repent, and he did so for weeks and weeks like a surge of the waves of the sea, crying out to God to save him, telling God that his life was His, asking God to take control of his life, confessing his sins, asking for forgiveness, asking for new life in Jesus Christ, asking for mercy for his wickedness and for his defiance and for his pride and self-glorification. And when truth came, it came strong and gashed him and knocked him down unto the bowing boards of his pride-buckled soul, and drown he did, resurrected unto life in Jesus Christ whereby thus did he from thence sail upon living waters.

HENRY OLDEN

Henry Olden was born in 1949 in Sioux Falls, South Dakota. Died in 1983 in Pocatello, Idaho. Henry was not known by many. But those who knew him got together when he died and came up with an epitaph that said:

That such a freight dispersed
from this soul
And that such bitter fruit turned good
Thus hath proved the working and the
Testifying of the Holy Spirit

ART FIELDRUNNER

Art Fieldrunner was born in 1922 in Detroit, Michigan. Went missing in 1956. Art told everyone he took character seriously. Most of the time he went down the road without going all over the place. His straightforwardness was, most of the time, without a slant. But sometimes he was, it seemed, unable to experience pleasure except in only the direst of circumstances. He gave much to his wife and son. When he went somewhere, sometimes he didn't tell his family where he was going. And sometimes he would go out at night and not come home for a long time, but his wife told his son that Jesus could find him in the darkness. His son saw him one time in the kitchen just standing there like he lost something, but he didn't seem to be looking for it. He liked doing things indoors but he smoked in the house and his wife didn't like that so she would want to take her son and go out a lot, but he didn't want to and told her to go places and he wouldn't go. Sometimes his wife and son would stay in the son's bedroom with the door open and read the Bible for a long time. His wife, one time, told their son about how Jesus is the Good Shepherd and that He loves everyone, but that maybe God did not know his dad and that his dad did not know Him and that he was therefore lost and wasn't one of His sheep, but to keep praying for dad that he become one.

TOM HEDGER

Tom was born in 1943 in Alden, New York. Died in 1999 in Allentown, Pennsylvania. Tom was abandoned by his mother at two years of age. Everyone always said that Tom had what could be called good morals, but that he never had boy-scout allegiance. Tom liked to say, "Of the mice, there are rats able to digest the filth." When Tom was thirty-five, he encountered the Lord. Three months later at his baptism he said, "I no longer feel surrounded by people that do not know the time on the clock of me." And he once said, "I know that for those in the kingdom of the Lord, mercy reigns in the town of hardship." From the point in which Tom believed the Gospel of Jesus Christ, he was on fire for God, and was thereby representative of a ruby in its radiant stance over the tranquility of perfect diamonds.

JOHN RADDER

John Radder was born in 1932 in Dallas, Texas. Died in 1992 in Birmingham, Alabama. John loved his teenage years. Shirtless days and braless nights. The older he got, the angrier he would get. And one time, when he was seventeen, in the middle of the town square where everyone was discussing a recent lecture, he yelled, "Brilliance doesn't stream from the mind but bursts forth from the heart when the heart isn't full of the lie." And he would also say things like, "An ambitious prince is too hesitant to become a king." He traversed the line of intellectual questioning to a kind of "animal-sense" plundering. He wrote a poem when he was seventeen:

If there should come a time, that I
Were to look inside and see no gain, the
Fire of my chest would begin to wane,
And, if that fire should become a flicker,
My self-worth should become but that
Much littler, leaving my heart to become
A most piddling source, and the world at
Hand, but an overwhelming force.

John believed that those who were able to translate daunting actualities into purposeful activities could not but be propelled into the excellence of life. He believed that every inhabitant of the world could function at the apex of life's allotment. John would walk the streets at a peculiar pace, venturing far like a displaced planetary wanderer looking for a spiritual standoff with a luminously-braided brain. He thought he had as many thoughts as there are stars. He thought he was as knowledgeable as man can be. That is, until the truth was in him. And when it was, God turned the rot of his being into a beautiful blossoming.

GUY TIDEWELL

Guy was born in 1915 in Chicago, Illinois. Died in 1987 in Chicago, Illinois. Guy was orphaned when he was two. A farming family that had moved to the city in 1912, adopted him. They raised him in the Word. Along with scripture, Guy remembered fondly the Spurgeon sermons. When Guy came of age, he began delivering newspapers. When Guy wasn't working, he was preaching on street corners. Drunk with the Holy Spirit, he talked much about corrupt fruit with its worms of wickedness ever squirming in the soil of unregenerate souls. Guy faced evil taunts daily. But the holy spirit comforted him. And the holy spirit, through Guy's street-corner ministry, changed the hearts of many. The demons knew him. Watched him daily in a most terrible assemblage. When Guy died, there was, in the town, a magnificent dirge over his passing. And those in the Faith, after the funeral, discussed the glory of God until dawn.

BILLY WELLSOUND

Billy was born in 1898 in Fremont, Nebraska. Died in 1957 in Los Angeles, California. Billy was like the sun. The distance it has from the world. The magnificence of its singular presence. The strength with which it affects us. Having walked with the cane of poetry on the fault of the world, Billy died footslogging up the incline of the diameter of his heart.

OLIVIA BRACER

Olivia was born in 1989 in Wood County, Wisconsin. Died in 2010 in Chicago, Illinois. Olivia justified her unraveling by making her child the source of her anguish. When one succeeded in coercing her into a conversational affair, her speech was a soft whispering of indecipherable sounds, for she knew that her soul may force her to beg. There was too much earth in her love. Though she spent most of her life trying not to remember the climb to the top to try to move forward, she yearned so much for praise that, to remain at giddy heights, she allowed a false self to be the one she wore. With her past ever threatening her present, eventually anguish bound her to her room, concealing her body but not her heart from being eaten away by an inconceivable wound.

REDDY FRIEND

Reddy was born in 1929 in Jackson, Mississippi. Died in 2003 in Austin, Texas. Reddy was very adamant about being right. His mother called it the religion of litigation. He was always upset that the lives of the majority seemed as stagnant as anemic worms. That people were ill with the sickness of calamitous griping. He didn't like that people thought a most splendid awareness is delegated to those who review the news of the soul, that only by the constant awakenings of new realizations should the scales of blindness be eternally shed. And that what in the day is a fluke in the night is a trial. Reddy thought people thought they were exempt from accountability and judgment. O how he wanted to become an inspired compassionate leader creatively power-learning to be able to better effect our future. He had a reoccurring dream where he backs up against a wall and the wall disappears and people are there to greet him, and he backs away and they raise their glasses to him, and when he reaches the opposite wall, he pushes at it until he can push no more then slowly crouches down into a posture that brings him as much comfort as a wall can bring. He was only ever attracted to that which the soul may take beyond the world. In 1999, four years before he died, Reddy made friends with a man from another state named Bill. This man was not a Believer. But the year Reddy died, one night in July, Bill and Reddy argued about truth until the sun came up. Bill argued that not only are men not without investigative leanings, but they are also not without the capability to know the truth, saying to Reddy, "You reason that objective truth exists, that its essence lies in some maker, some uncaused first cause. You find meaning where there is none. Man's purpose resides in his interpretation of purpose. The greatest in man is born out of the most chaotic of circumstances. Strife is imperative to grasp the full significance of the human experience. You are wrong to say that men are fallen, that they are, in need of redemption, and that atheism poisons the world." Then Reddy asked Bill, "Is it not your belief that man is random chaos, a disorderly order?" And Bill replied, "The soul, using your word, is but a furnace fed with the coal of false beliefs. Man is a composite of the elements of nature. He sheds like winter, ages like fire." Reddy followed with, "Bill, what you would call wrongdoing you wouldn't associate with sin; but whatever caused the atrocity, the abomination, has, the print of the fall and the mark of the devil. Bill, the world is the reflection of the sinful nature of man. You don't see the world as a cesspool? Do you think that we are merely dancing to our DNA?" "Bill, hear me on this: we abhor truth because we think that our rented intelligence supersedes the superintendent of the universe. We have been separated from God because of our sin. This is the link that has been broken. And here is the danger for the materialist: he grapples with what he believes some day will be grasped." While Bill sat silent and seemingly aggravated, Reddy read out of the Bible, sharing the Gospel of Jesus Christ, and ended by saying, "There can be no misalignment of the soul if exalted with the perfect alignment of the Word." They didn't end the night until the insects went to sleep. Five months later, Bill went to Reddy's house to tell Reddy that he had repented, and that he had been given the gift of belief, and that he knew that God was in control of him. But Reddy had died two months earlier. Bill spent the day with Reddy's wife and kids. Bill talked about all their conversations and arguments, and about how God had converted him. Bill, with the approval of Reddy's wife, wrote Reddy's epitaph:

Here lies Reddy Friend
He whose strength in Christ
Ran like the lion but proceeded like the
Delicacy of the lamb
Glory to the Triune God

AUGUST RED

August was born in 1938 in Tuscaloosa, Alabama. Died in 2013 in Uppsala, Sweden. August was present a way lucidity isn't, like a soul unobserved on the banks of creation. His mind was heavy with biblical knowledge. His deepness seemed to be a depth that could, couldn't reach. His hate of the world was his greatest strength. August spent the last thirty years of his life as a missionary in Sweden. The majority of the Swedes August encountered loved the world as much as August hated it. August and his wife evangelized all over. August saw the Lord working. Lives were changed. The night August died, there was R & R in hell.

DILLON POOL

Dillon was born in 1971 in Detroit, Michigan. Died in 2015 in New York City. Dillon was work-bent. Always striving. He would have reoccurring dreams of traveling to another dimension to rest. He was a solitary man, always struggling to make himself into a well-set self so that he may reemerge unbreakable against the actions of those of deficient morals. Dillon thought that from dauntlessly questioning without purpose or prejudice, every one of his interests and curiosities, that he would become deeply familiar with his own sensibilities. He thought that free will was the father of individuality, and that to look for one's purpose without having first attempted to discover oneself is to look for life in a region as bare as an old man's scalp. His heart was filled with lofty feeling. His mind swarmed with wonderful thoughts, and his being with exalted yearning. He came to believe that his soul basked in the vastness of the spiritual realm, eternally turning a metaphysical tan. He sometimes thought that what he felt was the boundless radiance gleaming out of the divinity of a holy existence. He saw himself as a forsaken genius. And he always thrusted himself into doing. For Dillon thought that if one does nothing towards becoming a "doing being," he may become eternally lost whereupon a once heavenly foundation may erode until it becomes a most ruinous atmosphere. He thought that burdens don't crush you as much as tell you who you are. For he thought that the heights a hero may reach, depends on his actions on the eve of the bottommost fall. He thought the agony of the soul was but a clash of the will. He thought that man was either a hellish heaven or a heavenly hell, but never solely one or the other. In his early twenties he thought he had been awakened like a slumbering god, whereupon he began to think his mind to be a space too big for the world to plug. A week after Dillon died, his brother found a journal with a single entry dated December 22nd, 2014, in which Dillon had written:

Anxious for purpose, I peer-out from the
Coffin of a body like a submarine, finding
Neither solace nor reason yet am drug
Along to explore the sights of the world
Never having control of my vessel.

EVAN MINT

Evan was born in 1941 in Xenia, Ohio. Died in 1975 in Aden, Yemen. Evan died on the Mission Field, bleeding the Gospel of Jesus Christ. And when Evan died, mortality cried whilst eternity smiled.

EDEN BRUSH

Eden was born in 1971 in Traverse City, Michigan. Went missing in 2015 in Detroit, Michigan. Some say Eden was pulled from her mother on the banks of the Sleeping Bear Dunes. Some say she was the seed of a woman warrior grown into the trunk of a hapless mother. And some say she was unable to withstand trauma like Pilot after the death at Golgotha.

PARKER UPFELL

Parker was born in 1940 in Savannah, Georgia. Went missing in 2002. Last seen in Rialto, California. Those who knew him best said he lived like a successful proprietor unfamiliar with his property. In his later years, the tomfoolery in which he partook seemed less and less like fun than persnickety distraction. When especially lonely, he became irritated with all kinds of bugs and trickles of sound. Parker seemed not broken enough to yield life. Or rather, he was not broken—correctly. Parker died of a heart attack at age sixty-two.

FENTON JACKSON

Fenton was born in 1950 in Dodge City, Kansas. Died in 2001 in Topeka, Kansas. Fenton was a very prideful man, grotesquely bejeweled like a festival animal. In his youth, he was ever torn with the abrasiveness of the thorns of rebellion. Streams of sin sprang forth amidst the fields of his mind, reaping countless crops of perversion. Thus, every harvest was a crop without a drop of ethical irrigation. His cousin once said of him, "His well was so deep and full of muck an angel couldn't slick him." Having been christened, at a young age, into the pornography business, and as many involved in such abominations find in themselves further inclinations for wicked obscenities, Fenton went further than you can imagine. In time, guilt ate at his lining like a piranha on a goldfish. Fenton knew his heart was but a cavity of pride and lust. And that the winds of evil drove the sails. As the blank inside of him was stuffed with the world, when the spiritual bullet of the true Gospel hit him (through an interaction with one of Fenton's neighbors), Fenton dropped to his knees in repentance, trembling. Fenton died of cancer at fifty-one years. Eight years before Fenton gave up the ghost, he was given the gift of belief in Jesus Christ, and by the Holy Spirit was born anew: the old man had died, and a new man arose in his place, carrying his cross unto death. Fenton's epitaph, written by his neighbor and closest friend, reads:

Man looks out through the windows of his pride and sees himself esteemed in glory. God looks upon man and says: because of my Son I will stay the axe at the girth of thy twisted trunk. I will give thee good fruits. I am the vine, and you are the branches, and I do not grow askew or uproot.

JAMIE SAXON

Jamie was born in Amsterdam in 1972. Died in Los Angeles, California in 2017. Jamie, from age twelve, was groomed to be a "party favor" for the rich. Every night was a grotesque display of illicit deeds. His life was a horrid wonderland of sexual indulgence for the elite. After his fourth role as an actor, Jamie was sacrificed to Moloch at Bohemian Grove.

GUY PEAKMIRE

Guy was born in 1912 in Springfield, Missouri. Died in 1983 in Kansas City, Missouri. Guy grew up under a renowned despot and in his youth took to a bottom feeding criminal and in his early adulthood distilled to a backwater tyrant like a mutating fish in a contaminated river. That was until he was Born Again and was thus given power over sin. Guy, for the rest of his life, sought to rightly divide the gospel of grace.

PERRY OVERMAN

Perry was born in 1964 in Rankin, Mississippi. Died in 2013 in Gary, Indiana. As a child, Perry fed on the meat of a most familiar buffet. But when Perry came of age, his way was the loosest of structures, a ramshackle soul driven by unintelligible bones. His red, raggedy garment hung loose on his body like the flag of brutality. Perry embraced the world. Every side. But at some point, he started to fall like a hot air balloon without fire. And the deeper Perry fell, the more he smote his mind with ungodly wants. He fell into an abysmal grief. It wasn't long until he made a pledge to die. And when he committed suicide, the ruler of the land of the dead came upon him like a black horizon.

TARWELL HOPEFOR

Tarwell was born in 1948 in Omaha, Nebraska. Died in 1972 in Sarasota, Florida. Tarwell forsook husbandry, striving in vain workmanship for lasting impression, impatient for the time of the world's recognition. The compass of his beliefs took him far outside the geography of truth. His heart had become the right kind for the world to notice. Soon enough the secret groups came to him with the most enticing delights. After many drug-fueled orgies, came the first prepubescent, but Tarwell refused. No one knows what happened to Tarwell.

DANE WARD

Dane was born in 1948 in Bristol, Rhode Island. Died in 1974 in Baltimore, Maryland. Dane thought one may see the beauty of God in the eyes of a wolf or come to know it from the love of a whore. His deathbed scene was not unlike a lurid, pulp magazine.

SLADE WELTE

Slade was born in 1980 in Bogota, Columbia. Died in 1986 in Cortez, Colorado. Slade went missing in 1985. Slade's body was found severely mutilated. And her pineal gland was removed.

COAXER SEEDTREE

Coaxer was born in 1901 in Bluefield, West Virginia. Died in 1953 in Tulsa, Oklahoma. With homespun intactness and unequivocal dutifulness, knowing that one knew right from wrong from the made-in-the-image-of God-knowledge of one's being, he thought the heart to be the most important tool in the human kit. He also thought that if his true identity were to become stunted, his dreams may evaporate, and thus shall become but the vague remembrances of a forgotten world. He followed the impulses that lead him to unknown destinations in hopes that he would be led out of the everyday. He wanted to be blessed with the kind of spiritual nourishment that makes one iron-strong in the Truth, and thus to be generating but the brilliant sparks of the sharpening of a continually renewed mind. But Coaxer didn't possess that which he professed. That was until he heard an hour-long sermon on Romans 7. From that point on, the Holy Spirit—having convicted Coaxer's heart to a full shattering, bringing about genuine repentance and true belief in Jesus Christ—continued to lead him in biblical truth. Coaxer loved to say, "The man that sees the world, even in a time of lesser wars, as a camp of dread, this man's eyes are open." And he also liked to say, "True bible teachers are a dying breed, and more than dire is our spiritual need."

ISABEL WEATHERWAY

Isabel was born in 1901 in Helena, Montana. Died in 1920 in Tombstone, Arizona. Isabel, an orphan, grew up in the Traveling Show. When she came of age, she ran headlong into the myth of the grandeur of one's dreams, ultimately unraveling from the fabric of time like a unicorn in fog.

ALICE WENT

Alice was born in 1974 in Labelle, Florida. Died in 2014 in Dulce, New Mexico. Alice was always doing night things at day places. The more she experienced, the more she sought. Influence taught her that self-realization sat on the highest seat on the spectrum of opportunity. And because such ambition is the evil that distorts the mind with thoughts of purpose, it wasn't long until she began to meditate. And through the guidance (deception) of her spirit guides (demons), she thought that she had come to achieve a higher state. There came to be something in her heart so bitter and vile and depraved . . . something darker than an African religion at midnight. Externally she was gaining, but internally imploding. It got to the point to where she could only ever be comfortable if she was standing in the middle of nowhere and there was nothing anywhere in every direction. Alice ended her days catatonic. A fantasy writer would later make a lot of money exploiting Alice by basing a character on her whom he called, both, "The Gatekeeper to the country of dreams," and, "A Watcher of the spiritual continuum."

TROY IDLE

Troy was born in 1939 in Arcadia, Wisconsin. Died in 1982 in Little Freedom, Wyoming. Troy was a heavy tender thing. He saw himself lagging far behind the caravan of intellect, but he knew he was an excellent frontline listener. He always said he was able to feel the sadness of those that had taken a beating so great that it could not but create a massive void within them. Troy had had an apprenticeship with loneliness but was on his way to becoming the foreman of isolation. People would surround him like an adulterer in a Muslim country. Accusations would leap hurriedly from their tongues, such that would Tyson his heart. Still, Troy's heart was heavy and blistered with love for all. Without a brother in Christ, his reliance on God was so total that it drove him to boldly proclaim the truth every waking hour, which the Holy Spirit honored with revival.

HUGO BETTY

Hugo was born in 1943 in Pittsburgh, Pennsylvania. Died in 2024 in Tokyo, Japan. Hugo was obsessed with immortality. He was a Futurist. Thought that we could transcend these "biological limitations." That human finitude is just a problem to be solved. Hugo would say things like, "The past is irrelevant," and, "To go beyond, we have to go beyond ourselves." Hugo's striving towards godhood is none other than the promise made by the Nachash in the Garden. Hugo's hope was to flee death by seizing God's rightful place as creator.

MIDNIGHT GENESIS

Midnight was born in 2017 in London, England. A panoramic view of the city is like an incomprehensible gadget. Midnight lives in a world as wicked as the heart of Nimrod, a city of practices as warped as a demonic liturgy, where workers work like mastered puppetry, junkies rove like emaciated jackals, and cats clean themselves like leprosy. The exactitude of the crosshairs of the abominably ambitious world-roving power-players are such, that they persuade innumerable threadbare denizen call-girls to mother-manipulate preteens so that the powerful may amuse themselves like the games of demented gods. Midnight is a threat to this world because of He who resides in her. For she is washed by the blood of the Lamb, and every branch of this evil system knows that the power of the God she worships, no power can withstand. Midnight knows that the cocoon of divine grace is the bed in which she will rest forever, and therefore fights to advance the kingdom of God by leading nightly a battle through prayer against the strongholds of evil influencing the masses to ghost themselves into an endlessly vivid, programmable universe of guaranteed dreams. Midnight's apartment is hued blue from the massive neon light hanging on the far wall in her Living Room, which reads: *your nature is the kind of slavery you can't escape from.* Midnight knew too much about human trafficking, murder, rape, all sorts of torture, pedophilia, satanic ritual abuse, and agony and despair: all the norm in a world ruled by the prince of the power of the air.

for we do not wrestle against flesh and blood, but against the rulers, against the authorities, against the cosmic powers over this present darkness, against the spiritual forces of evil in the heavenly places.

Eph 6:12

Midnight is fighting the good fight: sharing the Gospel; in constant prayer for revival; and is treading on scorpions and snakes with the authority given to her by the name that is above every name: Jesus Christ.

www.ingramcontent.com/pod-product-compliance
Lightning Source LLC
Chambersburg PA
CBHW061255040426
42444CB00010B/2383